BECOMING XKWIZIT

JOURNEY OF SELF-DISCOVERY

CARMELA MONTGOMERY

DEDICATION

This book is dedicated to all that have loved and lost. To everyone that has gone through the joys and pains of life. To everyone, it will be okay, things will work out. So live, love, learn and repeat.

ACKNOWLEDGEMENTS

I would like to thank my mother, who always encouraged us, pushed us to live our lives as fully and richly as possible. She showed such strength in the face of adversity; I've never forgotten that lesson.

I want to thank my sister for being such a great cheerleader and role model. You have always helped me stay motivated, and I'm so proud of the person you've become!

To my best friend in the whole world, thank you for always being there and keeping it real with me no matter what—friends like you are hard to find, so I want you to know that I appreciate our friendship.

I want to thank my love for your unwavering support and love during this journey. You have made me feel that I can do anything in life!

JOURNEY TO SELF-DISCOVERY

What is self-discovery? It's a constant discovery of who you are. It's a never-ending journey and though I will never fully understand, what I have realized is that as long as we are breathing, we will always be in a state of self-discovery.

Carmela is an artist and poet who delights in painting abstract art and writing poetry that reflects the human spirit. Her work is a delicate combination of passion, inspiration, imagination—and deep conviction.

Carmela is interested in creating ambiguous abstract art that blurs the lines between multi-dimensional realities. She paints and writes from a deep place where light meets dark and dark meets light. Her bold and vibrant paintings and words reveal the struggle, strength, and resilience of the human spirit. As an intuitive painter and writer, she is inspired by the emotions of the human spirit.

She hopes to inspire and empower people through her art and poetry.

Her uniquely personal approach to painting and writing reflects her own life experiences, which are both bold and vibrant. She believes that it is a person's intuition—that inner voice we all have—which speaks to us first of all. A reflection of our spiritual souls on the journey through life. She feels this vision shines through in what she creates as well!

I
N
T
R
O

We all have experiences that shape us and mold us into the people we are today. These events—whether good or bad—become a part of our DNA, shaping who we are as individuals.

My poems are about sharing my life experiences and hoping that someone out there can relate, feel comforted knowing they're not alone, and be encouraged to take steps within their own lives to make things better.

I'm not sure I will ever understand the meaning of life but knowing that helps me stay open to new experiences and learning.

My aim in writing this book is to inspire readers—and if it moves or inspires just one person, then I feel as though my purpose will have been fulfilled.

With that being said, let's get into it. This is my journey to self-discovery written in spoken word. Enjoy!

LIFE

YOONIR

We are all in the Matrix
surrounded by worldly illusions,
but we must continue to discover
who we are and what we are. You
and your purpose are divine.

Life is a journey that we all embark on from the moment we are born. It's a journey that can take us through many twists and turns, highs and lows, and unexpected surprises. Each of us has a unique path that we must follow, and it's up to us to make the most of the time we have.

As we journey through life, we encounter challenges that test our strength and resilience. We face moments of self-doubt and uncertainty, but we learn to push through and overcome our fears. We discover that our failures can be our greatest teachers and that our mistakes can lead us to new opportunities.

The journey of life is not always easy, but it is in those moments of difficulty that we learn the most about ourselves. We learn to be patient, kind, and compassionate. We learn to be grateful for the people in our lives and for the experiences that shape us.

As we journey through life, we grow and evolve. We learn from our mistakes, gain wisdom, and develop a deeper understanding of ourselves and the world around us. And at the end of the day, what really matters is not what we've accomplished or how far we've gone, but the memories we've made, the people we've touched, and the legacy we leave behind.

In the end, the journey of life is a beautiful and profound experience. It is a journey of growth, learning, and self-discovery. It is a journey that we all must take, but it is up to us to make the most of it. So, let us cherish every moment, embrace every challenge, and never forget the beauty and wonder of the journey of life.

Life is a beautiful mess but it's also amazing. Life is hard but also full of fun and laughter.

Life is confusing but also so rewarding.

Life is a roller coaster of emotions, but that's what makes it so beautiful.

Life can be so hard and painful at times, but it also has its moments of pure joy and happiness.

Life is full of ups and downs, but it's still worth living every single day and this is something I have learned along the way.

This journey I am on has taught me that sometimes it's okay to cry and feel sad, but there will be better days ahead. It has taught me that sometimes it's okay to be angry and hurt, but there will also be moments of pure joy and happiness in your life. It has taught me that no matter what happens in life or how many times I fall down, it's important to keep going and never give up. It has taught me that life is worth living, even through its ups and downs.

Life has taught me that it's important to live in the moment, because you never know what tomorrow will bring. It has taught me that there are people out there who will love and support you no matter what happens. It has taught me to be kind and compassionate with myself, as well as others around me.

Life has taught me to be strong and resilient, even in the face of adversity. It has taught me that no matter how hard things get, there is always light at the end of the tunnel.

LIFE

We are all born alone and will leave this world alone. On this journey of life, you will have ups and downs and at times feel like you are being turned all around.

Live life to the fullest with joy in your heart and gratitude on your tongue because these lives given are all on loan.

Life is an experience, and we must gain an understanding that life is going to happen whether we want it to or not.

Life is not perfect but this life we experience is worth it.
Be aware of the serpents that will cross your path; they are only here to steal your peace, joy and sometimes your life.

Life is a decision, and you must live it without permission from those who try to place restrictions on who you are. You are the light that shines bright lighting up the darkest of nights.

Only allow those who contribute to your spirit and purpose into your sacred space.

Some are only here to keep you distracted from bearing the fruits of your purpose by having you in a state of constant confusion with their own self-induced delusions and circus act of illusions.

Life is full of beautiful moments that will carry you in moments of strife. They will help restore and replenish your spirit while you are on this journey of discovery.

Have gratitude each and every day.
Live with intention and listen to your intuition for it will guide you to your destiny while keeping the vultures from swooping on your head.

Life is what you make it. Life is lessons and blessings.
So, learn from those lessons so that you can move on and receive the blessings.

Life is beautiful and a mess. So, participate fully.
Life is full of wonder. So, explore it with an open mind and heart.

Life is unexpected. So, stay strapped in and enjoy the ride.

Love the life given for it will never be another given the same way again.

UNSPEAKABLE

You did the unspeakable to me.
As my family you were supposed to be one of the ones who protected me.

That day a part of me died.
I held the trauma inside until I almost died.
The pain and shame would not go away no matter how many times I cried.

You Pedo, I was only nine and you used me for whatever sadistic thoughts in your mind and I believed it was all my fault, you sadistic freak.

I carried the burden you placed upon my shoulders like boulders.
I learned that day the world was colder than I could ever imagine.

I had to learn this harsh truth not from the outside world, but from the one within.

Part of my childhood ruined and forgotten, blacked out cause my mind and body wanted to block out the trauma you place upon me.

Sometimes I wonder who I would've been if it never happened.
Growing up wishing I was somebody else, so it didn't happen to me but I'm here despite of what you did to me.

Despite how many times your demons tried to kill me since they thought they had dominion over me but I'm still standing cause I got the Divine within me.

Over many suns and moons, I have healed these wounds that were stuffed deep down inside.

I had to take the time to work on me and that meant forgiving you to start the healing process of me. That's why I will always shine.

I had to release your energy and spirit from mine.
I had to release the trauma hold so that I could take control of my life.

I release you completely and I take my power back and I will let the Divine deal with you and the karma you got owed back.
With no hate in my heart, I wish you well.

TRAUMA

I am fading away, like a memory of a distant dream, a forgotten melody. I am fading away, like a memory that refuses to stay. It has taken hold of me, and now I am just a shell of who I used to be.

It hit me hard, like a raging storm. It tore me apart, left me broken and worn. I tried to hold on, I tried to be brave, but the pain was too much, it felt like I couldn't be saved.

My mind is a maze, my thoughts trapped in a haze. I can't seem to find my way, and now I am starting to decay.

The darkness creeps in, like a disease, it spreads within, and I am consumed by the pain, as I try to fight, but it feels all in vain.

The memories haunt me, they never let go. The nightmares come back, they always know the triggers are there, they never fade. I'm trapped in this hell, my mind's betrayed.

I try to push the thoughts away but they always seem to find a way to creep up on me when I'm alone. It's like I'm trapped in my own home.

I feel like I'm fading away, like a picture that's slowly turning gray. The colors that once shown so bright, are now dull and lifeless in my sight.

But even as I fade, I still cling to the hope that's not yet frayed. The hope that one day, I will be okay, and I'll rise from the ashes of yesterday. For I know that there is a fire burning deep within my soul fighting for me to hold on.

For in the darkness, even the smallest flame can guide me out of the dark even though trauma has left its mark.

17
TO
THE
HEAD

The wounds are just too deep, the pain wakes me out of my sleep.
It feels like the world has turned its back on me and left me to pick up the pieces of my life others have broken.

I want these thoughts and feelings to go away, so I take it to the head to numb the pain inside and stop these memories from playing on repeat in my head. Why I feel so weak? Why does my life seem so bleak? Why does it feel like no one wants me even around?

I suffer in silence while the world goes on. No one sees me, no one knows the tears I cry, wishing I could just fade away into the abyss of the night sky where I'm at peace.

I am angry, I am sad, I am hurt, I feel abandoned, I feel betrayed, and I don't know what to do with all of these feelings, so I take it to the head to numb the pain but when it wears off the pain returns again and again, and I repeat the cycle every weekend.

I am broken and need someone to help me, but no one can help me when everyone around me can't even help themselves. We are all broken looking to escape this life we didn't ask to be a part of.

I am self-destruction in real time and I'm only hurting myself so there is no crime, so I take it to the head until I'm numb so I can sleep in peace and block out the shadows that torture me in the light and the dark. I don't know why peace seems to evade me. So, I created my peace at the bottom of the bottle quite easily; this is where I found comfort even if it was temporary.

I need to stop before the next chapter in my life because if I continue it would be a crutch I'd use for the rest of my life. The constant smell of alcohol is making me sick; I think it's the universe creating a way for me to get out this cycle before my world comes crashing down like a ton of bricks. My inner self telling me I need to quit before I'm in a situation and can't get out of it, but how do I stop these thoughts and feelings in my head?
I guess I'll figure it out eventually. Until then I'll just take this to the head.

DONOR

You left me alone, with nothing but memories of broken promises and lies.

Where were you when I needed you most? When I cried out in the night, when I struggled and fought, when I needed a hand to hold, when I needed a protector. Where were you when I needed you?

You were a ghost, a shadow in the back of my mind, a fading memory of what could have been, a void that I could not fill or find. You became a wound that would not heal.

I waited and hoped for you to come around, but you never showed. You were nowhere to be found. I yearned for your love, your guidance and care but instead all I got was broken promises and silence from a man that didn't care.

Reminders of the pain and the hurt, the abandonment and the loss, the burden of your neglect. For you, I have no respect, for the love I once had for you is now lost.

To the man who left before he began, who disappeared like smoke in the wind. This is a message for my donor, whose absence left a void within. You said you'd be there, but you never came, leaving me to suffer alone with a pain you caused.

You had a choice, but you chose to leave—to turn your back on your own blood. I'll never understand how could you believe that your absence would do me any good?

My mom had to do it all, she carried the weight and refused to fall. You were too busy, too selfish to participate in the raising of your creation.

Your absence was like a knife, cutting me deep. A wound that would never fully heal, no matter how much I wept. Your face eventually erased. Etched in memory, like a distant blur, once so clear, now hazy and unclear. Days turned into weeks, weeks into years, and until this day your face is still unclear. A stranger is what you are to me.

I used to wonder where you were, if you'd remember me if you saw me— his child, his blood, his miss—but all I'm left with is the emptiness of you not being around, but your legacy of neglect and abandonment will live on in my mind.

But I've learned to survive, in spite of your neglect. I've found my own strength. So, go ahead and keep running from your own reflection. For I am strong and resilient, despite absence, and I'll continue to grow, be victorious without your applause.

STILL
HERE

It's raining in my head; I think I'm better off dead.
This pain and torment are too much to take and too many haunting memories in my head. I see no end in sight for me. These thoughts and memories are consuming me from the inside, out. No one seems to hear my cries.

The first cry for help was at the age of 14, sitting in the dean's office, numb with no feeling inside, asking a classmate for a pair of scissors so I could end it all. It was my first cry for help out loud, but no one wanted to know or ask why.

So, my cry for help went unheard, So I closed my mouth and myself off to the world and never uttered another word. Showing this type of weakness to the world was not allowed, I had to put on the mask to hide my face, speak no word of this and maintain my space.

I learned to wear this mask daily, never let the world see me in this debilitating pain that left me constantly drained. The immense torment was literally driving me insane.

With sheet in hand, I began to pull. With tears streaming down my face, I pulled. With breath restricting I pulled tighter and tighter; all I knew is that I wanted to live and die at the same time. If I could just disappear for a moment, where the pain fades and these intrusive thoughts and memories I could evade. All I wanted was to be saved.

I was a slave to the shadows that haunted me, bound and shackled to their whipping post. It felt like the world around me treated me with contempt, so I made attempt after attempt and became half of the someone I used to be, now I'm just a faded memory drifting in and out of consciousness unaware of who I am or supposed to be.

I had to find the strength to live and know within myself I had something to give that's why I'm still here because my spirit refuses to die. I'm still here because no matter how dark it got the light within me still flickered.

I had to find love for myself, apologized to the younger me and understand my past is not my future, it's what helped save me, but it took me going to therapy to get the tools needed to fight the shadows that had me shackled and bond, now I could fight back without losing my crown.

I discovered my purpose was greater than my intentions to leave and through grace and mercy I now believe so, I make sure I give gratitude now rather than later by living my life to the fullest. All blessings due to the creator.

Been operating in a state of survival since I was nine.
Don't nobody understand what's going on in my mind.
Why can't this world be just a little more kind.
I used to drown my woes and sorrows into alcohol and wine.

At some point I had to change my state of mind.

I was self-destructing in real time, and no one even noticed my cry for help. I
then realized I was in this all by myself.
So, I stayed in a state of survival to protect myself.

Always wishing I was somebody else and maybe tomorrow somebody else.
Hoping I can make it right within myself, but world doesn't allow you to be
yourself, so you end up losing your sense of self then down the line having to
go back and re-find yourself.

Fighting the demons passed down through the generations because keeping
secrets was better than dealing with the harsh reality. So, I stayed in a state of
survival instead of healing.

The thought of no longer being in this world was very appealing, but I made the
decision to stay several times over even though deep down I just wanted it to
be over so the pain would go away, and I could for once feel okay.

So, I had to change my state of mind, forget what the world has to say and do
things my own way.

In my own way I found peace within me which has allowed me to thrive in this
world instead of just survive. I had to change my state of mind and though it
took some time I have now reclaimed my time.

I take back what has been stolen from me.
I take back my energy and light.
I take back my power and my strength.
Most importantly, I'll take back my life.

S
U
R
V
I
V
A
L

I've been broke, not a dime to my name, almost homeless.

Almost losing my life while going to see someone who lost their life. Doing 360 degrees across a highway will put a lot of things into perspective.

Then losing two of my family members within a two-week period reminds me ain't nothing promised.

They say life is hard but what they fail to tell you it's like building a house out of grains of sand.

As I walk through this unforgiving land it's my mind and heart I try to maintain and tame.

This world will break you down if you let it, but I refuse.

Now look into my eyes: don't you see the spark and the flame? So, pardon me while I burst into flames.

I've been lied on, cheated on, talked about and mistreated, but I stand on my own two doing what I got to do to stop the haters from walking over me.

So, I stay true to myself and hold my head up and make my own destiny because I refuse to run and hide from the cold harsh words of others, so I put on my jacket and keep on walkin why they keep on talkin getting their feet dirty in the messes.

I could easily fall by the way side and let this world corrupt me, drive me insane but there ain't nothing in this world that would make me sell my soul to be something I am not because everything I'm not makes me everything I am.

So, pardon me while I burst into flames.

**S
T
R
O
N
G
E
R**

Winds have knocked me down, but I got up and moved on. Oceans have tried to drown me but instead I swam. So many snakes in my path Lord only knows why I didn't stick around for the aftermath because what consumes your heart consumes your life.

You can't hold me down.
I will not run.
I will not hide, and I will not back down.
I will survive any situation, limitation, and temptation.

Hesitaters and procrastinators better known as hate and haters will get knocked the hell down when in my pathway.

So, pardon me while I burst into flames and rise like the Phoenix from the ashes because what don't kill me only makes me stronger.

BALANCE

Spiritually and mentally, I embark on a journey one foot in front of the other.

I try to keep my balance from shifting from left to right, trying not to fall into the darkness of night.

I stop and finally open my eyes; I get out of my own way and stop walking blinded by pride.

So, I walk this road alone in spite of the dangers ahead. I do what I have to do to get to where I want to be.

As my head spins around I wonder is that me or this earth rotating on its axis trying to confuse me?

It's the strength I hold within that keeps my feet grounded, belief and confidence in myself but I stay grounded.

I die over and over again to reborn into one who seeks what thy heart needs and wants and not what I can get.

Time is ticking and I'm not going to be left behind.

It's life that makes people go insane because they tired of the hurt and pain with the struggle to make it daily, but they smile and do what they have to do to get to where they need to be.

Spiritually and mentally, we all embark on a journey. One foot in front of another trying to keep our balance.

THE CYCLE
OF
HARD LESSONS

LISTEN

Some relationships improve us and make us stronger, while others can be bad for our self-esteem or give rise to other problems.

I was in a relationship that broke me. It was mentally and emotionally abusive, and I didn't even realize it until it was too late; like most people, I had been blinded by love and my own insecurities—ignoring so many red flags along the way.

I stayed in the relationship because I wanted to believe that it was going to get better. And when you love someone, it's easy to overlook their flaws and make excuses for them. We all have a breaking point—and if you've ever been in an unhealthy relationship, then you know what mine was like: I was depressed and anxious, felt worthless. They never gave me compliments; I had to constantly ask them if they found me attractive, liked being with me, or expressed affection.

A partner who truly loves you should not put limits on or try to change who you are. He or she may give advice, but a good partner will respectfully listen to your side of things and be willing to compromise with you—not undermine your dreams by comparing them with others. Your partner should always treat you with respect, never talking down to you or making you feel unworthy; they should bring peace—not chaos —into your life.

If someone consistently puts you down and makes it seem that all the problems are your fault, they're not good for you. You will eventually have to decide what is more important: holding onto something that you should never have had in the first place or your mental state.

My therapist diagnosed me with severe depression and PTSD, which were the result of trauma I had experienced in my childhood. My current relationship was also making things worse for me by exacerbating my symptoms.

It got so bad that I had to put my phone on vibrate, because the sound of their ringtone would trigger such anxiety in me. Until this day, my phone is still set on vibration when it rings or makes another noise.

Trauma and abuse can change your behaviors short term and long term. I have developed many triggers, but through self-relaxation techniques like meditation as well as counseling—I am in a much better place now. I also learned that I had to take time for myself—this was important in order to fully recover. I still have triggers today, but they are not as bad as they used to be. I now have the tools to cope with my triggers, and I am able to manage my anxiety. It is important to take time for yourself, especially if you are going through a hard time. I know that many people think that taking time for ourselves is selfish—but it's not! It is important to take care of ourselves before we can help others.

It is not selfish to work on yourself, and your partner should never make you feel that way. Taking the steps needed to remove yourself from an unhealthy situation should never be deemed as a betrayal by anyone. If your partner is making you feel like you are "selfish" for taking care of yourself, then it is time to reevaluate the relationship. If you are being made to feel bad about taking time for yourself—especially if that person is someone who claims to love and care about you—then it may be time to let go.

When an abusive partner realizes that you're no longer under their control, they will often try to regain power by acting more aggressively towards you. They will do everything in their power to try to make you feel as though you need them and that no one else would ever want you, making it seem like the problem is always with you. If you are feeling like this, it is important to remember that it isn't true.

You are a special person who deserves love and respect, no matter what anyone else says. If your partner constantly puts you down, belittles your accomplishments or tells you that you aren't good enough for them—then they don't deserve your time, energy or love. If you are feeling like this, it is important to remember that it isn't true. You are a special person who deserves love and respect. You are worthy and shouldn't let anyone make you feel otherwise. Point blank period!

After returning home from a trip, I reflected on my life and decided that if I didn't make some changes soon, it would be too late.

I started to meditate and work through my past traumas. I began asking myself those difficult "why" questions, like: Why do I have abandonment issues? Why is it so hard for me to let people go? Why am I so insecure? Why don't I love me (whichever version of that is true)?

Over the course of several months, I was forced to confront every traumatic event in my past. I had to have that talk with my inner child—the vulnerable part of myself who'd never been allowed healing or peace. I had to face the many demons that lurked and thrived in that darkness. I had to dig down deep and pull out all of the negative energy that had latched onto me over the years—that was no easy feat, believe me! Being in this place wasn't easy; it was one of hardest things I ever had done.

Learning to love myself was not an easy task, but once I learned that it is possible to fall in love with yourself, I understood that no other relationship could ever be as important. I removed all the barriers that once prevented me from seeing clearly. I asked the powers that be to remove people and things—in particular those who no longer served my mental or emotional wellbeing but were detrimental in maintaining it —from my life. I began doing daily affirmations to start my days in a positive way.

I AM STRONG

I AM INTELLIGENT

I AM COURAGE

I AM POSITIVE VIBRATIONS

I AM LIGHT

I AM SUCCESSFUL

I AM WORTHY

I AM XKWIZIT

And so, I began writing a list of affirmations, along with another list of what I would and wouldn't allow myself to accept.

I will not tolerate confusing words, actions, or behaviors.

I will not allow or tolerate destructive, demeaning, or insulting actions/words from anyone.

I will not allow anyone to make me feel inadequate.

I will not let anyone, or anything rob me of the joy and peace that should be a part of my life.

I will not allow anyone to stop me from speaking my mind
.
I will not allow people to treat me in any way they please.

I will not let anyone make me feel insecure about my choices.

I will not let anyone steal my energy and light.

I will not allow anyone to cross my personal boundaries.

I will stop giving water to situations that are already dead or dying.

I will do whatever it takes to safeguard my inner peace.

I keep these lists as reminders that I am worthy and to always move forward—so old insecurities and people don't creep back into my life.

Now that I've ended my relationship, most of the anxiety caused by our connection have dissipated. I feel like a burden has been lifted off me—like a heavy cloud evaporating from above me.

In the end, I wish them no ill will and all the best. The lessons I learned from this relationship were life changing. Old sayings like "some people are only in your life for a season" hold so much truth—I had to learn how to stop holding on to those who were seasonal relationships.

It's cloudy outside but not as cloudy as my head.
Wishing I could just lay here in this bed and forget everything that you said.

Part of me being angry and the other part feeling hopeless and afraid.
You feeling hatred and betrayed and enslaved by your own feelings and dealings
with your soul.

Having memories on repeat in my head like a broken record, lying here hoping
and praying one day you would truly see me.

Despite all of your dealings in life you say you are trying yet hearing the words "I
don't know" cut like a knife through my heart and soul.
They say the first cut is the deepest and I'm so knee deep in this.

Hoping one day you would open your eyes and heart and love me the way that I
needed but you constantly pretended to make progress just to recede it with time.

I'm not here to play games or place blames.
I am here to spark flames and help you push through all of your pain and make
sure our picture stayed in that frame, but I guess again I'm the one to blame.

I accepted your bare minimum thinking it was the best you could do.
Blinded by my insecurities you played on my insecurities and past traumas and
wanted me to medicate so that you could continue to manipulate.

I put loving you over loving me, and loving you was killing me slowly not wanting
to continue this hurt I find myself repeating, "Fool me once shame on you. Fool
me twice shame on me."

I had to hit rock bottom for the veil to fall. No longer mixing my dreams and
wishes with reality I now see you and your many changing faces while you admit
to being the devil's daughter. Now I realize you was just a test here to cause
chaos and disorder.

You were the hardest love lesson I ever learned that nearly cost me my life but
now I stand stronger realizing no one will ever love me like me.

R
E
A
L
I
Z
E
D

G
A
S
L
I
G
H
T
E
R

You are a master of manipulation, twisting and turning reality, making me feel insane with every strategic word you spoke.

You are a master of deceit, who wears a clever guise. Your words are like poison, seeping in, twisting and turning reality, a darkened spin, a victim of your own twisted mind, lost in your own maze, trying to find.

Your goal was to always control with subtle tactics; forever calculating and cruel, using my weaknesses as a tool. You played with my emotions like puppets on a string. Leaving me lost, confused and wondering.

Say that I'm overreacting, when you are the one that was always strategically attacking. Making me feel like I'm the one to blame, causing me to feel so much shame.

You played dangerous games with my mind leaving me feeling lost and confused, and doubting the things I once knew. A cruel charade, a villain, a monster, a masquerade, your words like daggers, cutting deep, leaving scars, and wounds that won't allow sleep.

Fooled by your deceitful allure, you were the devil of my time, leaving me in a endless cycle of depression and anxiety.

But I rose up and took my power back. I started trusting in myself and in my own mind. I stood up strong, and held my ground, and I refused to let you bring me down, for I am more than what you could see.

So, I walked away, and left what once was behind, a gaslighter's words and twisted mind.

A poison creeping through my veins. Inhale the air, tainted and stale, a poison that seeps through every veil. A silent killer, lurking unseen; a toxic substance, viciously attacking me.

I breathe it in, I swallow it down. Laced with toxins I can't perceive. They seep into my heart and skin with no consideration.

My body weakens, my mind grows dim as the poison spreads from deep within. I feel its grip, its cruel embrace a silent killer, with a unassuming face.

No antidote, no cure in sight. Just the constant battle, of wrong and right. A life lived, with a constant fear of the poison's power, forever near.

I feel it coursing through my blood, a toxic, deadly stream, a silent killer, like a flood, that steals away my dream.

My body is a battlefield, the poison always winning, a chronic exposure, unrevealed, my health forever thinning.

The world around me seems so bright, but I can't escape this pain. The poison that has taken flight and left me with no gain.

I try to resist, to fight the tide, but the toxins cling, and won't subside. My life slowly drained, my future bleak, as the toxic substance continues to make me weak.

Longing for cleaner air to breathe. I gather up my strength and courage, to walk away and save myself from your toxicity, once all-consuming now faded away. With every exhaling breathe, your venomous words, no longer heard my mental state no longer blurred.

Shedding the weight of your abuse and all of your toxic words. The pain and hurt, no longer affect me. I'll embrace the light that shines within and leave behind the pain that's been. For I deserve a love that's pure and true now that I have broken free from you.

BOND

We are all bonded by the two parts of our existence. The physical and spiritual. At times both working together in harmony and other times fighting against each other to survive.

I gotta look in the mirror.
I can't look in the mirror.
Take a look in the mirror.

I gotta look in the mirror.
I can't look in the mirror.
Take a look in the mirror.

I see the reflection of me or who I think I am or supposed to be.

Unsure of what I see.
I hang my head thinking to myself, have I forgotten me?

Take a look in the mirror.

I force myself to lift my head with tears flowing from my eyes as every part of my being cries.

Don't put yaself through it cause ya about to go through it.

Too much to handle we can't, I mean I can't, I mean you can't handle the truth.

The truth is that you are unloved by you.

Just turn and walk away and all of this emotional turmoil you're feeling will go away.

Take a look in the mirror.

Stop all this hesitation and take a look in the mirror.
Face yourself and see who you really are on the inside.

Don't fear what you see just be still and embrace me.

Look me in the eyes with conviction and tell me you love me, you love all of me despite all my faults, secrets and lies.

Look me in the eyes and say it.
Say I am worthy; worthy of me, myself, and I in this reflection and know that I am worthy of you and you of me.

Look me in the eyes and tell me I am beautiful.
Put that on repeat cause I need to hear and feel this each and every time we meet.

With me looking at me I stand in the stillness with tears flowing from my eyes like rivers and streams I tell myself I need this as I lay aside the pride within me.

I look into my eyes passed the physical with the understanding that this next step is critical in my journey of finding love of me through the process of healing, realizing this is what my soul has been needing and missing.

I breathe in deep, let go and say

I love you.
I am not my past mistakes.
I forgive you.
I am worthy of the love I give.
You are beautiful.
I am beautiful.
I am the reflection of beauty because I am love, light and worthy of the love within me.

BAGGAGE

Been carrying around this baggage full of trauma for decades from childhood to adulthood. Walking around this life feeling misunderstood and amazed I'm standing here today despite the pain I've endured.

It's heavy and weighing me down; I can't keep fighting the current, the sharks and this bag. If I don't do something now, I'm going to drown deep into the depths of no coming back.

At this point it's now or never cause this fate I cannot accept. I need to get this weight off my back. Mentally and physically, I can't let my past trauma be the demise of me.

So, I start cutting the straps of insecurity, self-doubt and fear so that I can gain mental dexterity. So, I can mentally prepare for the long journey ahead of me.

I cut the straps of illusions, hallucinations, and misinterpretation so that I can see more clearly. I need to stay focused on healing the inner child within. I can't let all this baggage keep me from my win.

I cut the straps of people and things that no longer serve me, miscommunication, procrastination, and past failures so that I can pull from the strength and determination I have always had inside me.

I fight my shadows into submission because they no longer have a place here.
I had to save myself from myself and become my own knight in shining armor.
Releasing all the years of trauma and anger I had pushed deep down inside me so that I could finally be free from the baggage that weighed me down.

Now I embrace this beautiful thing we call life with arms wide open.

ANXIETY

Energy building inside of me with no place to go.
It's like a stirring in my body, my mind and soul.
I can't explain what it is, just the feelings that I'm feeling deep down inside.

It's like being tossed and turned on the stormy seas with the waves constantly crashing into me, taking my breath away from me.

With my mind racing with no finish line in sight functioning but not functioning at the same time. I know it's hard to explain but I hate this feeling that
I'm feeling inside.

It's disrespectful and inconsiderate, coming and going as it pleases, disrupting my light causing it to flicker. Heck I don't know, I can't pinpoint the trigger.

Feeling like I need to scream to make it go away but no matter what I do, it seems to be making all of its intentions to stay without my say.

It's like its playing tug of war with my insides, taking me along for the ride and yes, I am tired—tired of fighting a source I cannot see but I find strength in knowing this won't get the best of me.

I breathe in deep, exhale and repeat.
I breathe in deep, refocus my mind, exhale and repeat.
I refuse to suffer in silence and accept defeat from the faceless man.
This will not control or get the best of me.
No longer weak. I got mighty strength inside of me.

I am not a sufferer of this.
I am a conqueror of this of which we cannot see.
This thing we call anxiety.

Nights like this
Nights like this
wishing I could go away.
Cosmic universe come take me away.

Nights like this
Nights like this
wishing I could go away.
Cosmic universe come take me away.

Nights like this I lay in bed staring out the window
Wishing I was in another place.
Floating amongst the stars and no one can see my scars just lay back
and listen to these melodic bars.

Nights like this
Nights like this
wishing I could go away.
Cosmic universe come take me away.

Nights like this
Nights like this
wishing I could go away.
Cosmic universe come take me away.

Nights like this I lay in bed.
I let the tears flow out my eyes and wash away all my pain.
I lay in the comfort of knowing tomorrow will be a better day.
But for now, I will lay here in this bed watching myself float amongst
the stars to get away from

Nights like this
Nights like this
wishing I could go away.
Cosmic universe come take me away.

Nights like this
Nights like this
wishing I could go away.
Cosmic universe come take me away.

N
I
G
H
T
S

L
I
K
E

T
H
I
S

HIGH TOLERANCE

People who know me well say that I tolerate much more than I should. They've told me my tolerance for the intolerable is high, and they can't imagine putting up with what I've dealt with in my past. During my journey of self-discovery, I had to pause and ask myself why I've tolerated so much in the past. So, in asking "why?"—I began uncovering a lot of deep-rooted issues from when I was younger that needed healing.

Facing myself was not easy, it was dark and sad. But I knew that I couldn't move on in life without allowing myself to be truly vulnerable with myself. When I allowed myself to be vulnerable and face my shortcomings, I was able to overcome many of the obstacles that had been holding me back. I did not leap into this process. I had to take several steps—mentally, emotionally, and spiritually preparing myself as best I could—before deciding that it was time for me move forward. So, I began to ask myself why so that I could gain an understanding of what caused me to be the way that I am. I began to realize that I had been suppressing my emotions for many years. I was afraid of what would happen if I allowed myself to feel how I really felt. Once this happened, I found that there were many other things in my life that needed addressing as well. It wasn't easy facing myself and all of the things that had happened in my past, but it was worth it because once I did so, I began to feel better about myself and my life. I was able to forgive myself for the things that had happened in my past, as well as those who had hurt me. This helped me move forward with my life with a new sense of freedom and optimism.

Why do I allow people to treat me badly?

- Because I am afraid of losing them

Why am I afraid of losing someone?

- Because I feel that's the best I can get

 Why do I feel like that is the best I can get?

- Because I feel unworthy

 Why do I feel unworthy/unattractive?

- Because I feel like nobody wants me or thinks I am attractive

Why do I feel unworthy/unattractive?

- Because I always felt invisible

 Why have you always felt invisible?

- Because no one ever noticed me

Why no one ever noticed me?

- Because my sister was light skin and pretty

Why did I feel my sister was prettier?

- Because I was always told that she was prettier by the world

W H Y ?

Why do I hate not knowing?

- Because I always feel like it's my fault, and I want to fix the problem

Why do I feel like it's always my fault?

- Because I feel inadequate

Why do I feel inadequate?

- Because I feel like I can't do anything right

Why do I feel like I can't do anything right?

- Because I have no confidence

Why do I have no confidence?

- Because I feel like I am always being criticized and critiqued.

Why don't I love myself?

- Because I feel worthless

Why do I feel worthless?

- Because I've lost all confidence in myself

Why did I lose all confidence in myself?

- Because I was bullied
- Because I was abandoned
- Because I was sexually assaulted

Why was I bullied?

- I don't know

Why was I abandoned?

- Because my dad didn't want me

Why was I sexually assaulted?

- I don't know

These were some of the hard questions I needed to ask myself in order to get at the root cause of my issues. Some questions may never be answered—and that's ok, because once I determined my why's, I decided to face the "whys" of my past and ask myself whether those reasons should shape who I am. I realized that I needed to make peace with my past, but not be held captive by it. And so, I made a conscious decision to forgive my past and move forward.

ACCEPTANCE

Acceptance is patience in the understanding that life is and will always be forever changing.

The ups and downs the twists and turns in the chaotic space we call life which sometimes cuts deep into your inner being like a knife.

Stand still in the midst and resist the urge to be consumed. Allow your body and mind to breathe and just be.

Know that you are the light to the darkness, the balancing scale between the divine masculine and feminine energy. Two worlds held within one spirit.

Acceptance is understanding that your journey is yours and yours alone. No one is coming to save you from yourself but you.

Face the darkness within and fight to the death and let go of the old you that was no good to you and emerge anew.

Stand in your truth and let go of all that is not conducive to you and your light.

Acceptance is understanding the space you are in today won't be the space tomorrow so trust the process and go with the flow and accept who you are in the here and now and move forward and grow. Stay humble in your quest and let no one deter you and remember acceptance is not complacency; it is an action of consenting to receive who you are and where you are in this moment.

TURNING POINT

POINT

THE TRANSITION

TRANSITION

Transitions are not without struggle, but we must go through the storm in order to grow. We have to dig deep within, face our fears and ourselves. Don't give up, don't give in or give out and you will emerge victorious.

It is often during times of transition that we must struggle the most in order to grow. We have to dig deep within ourselves, face our fears and be honest about who we are. We must be willing to look at our pasts and acknowledge the mistakes we've made. We need to learn from these experiences in order to move forward. It is during this process that we can come out on the other side of the tunnel into a place of peace and understanding. We need to know that even though our lives may have been filled with difficulty, there is always hope for a brighter future.

During my time of transition, I had to isolate myself from the world and everyone in it. It was something inside me that was pushing me—almost forcing me—to take this time to work on myself. I had to learn to be okay with being alone, and I had to accept the fact that I couldn't control what people thought or did. The only thing I could control was myself and my thoughts. In order to get through this time in my life, I had to let go of the past and focus on the future. I had to accept what was happening to me and realize that there were no other options besides accepting it and moving forward into a better place. I had to realize that I was in the driver's seat of my own life and no one else could make me happy. The only person who could make me happy was myself.

During your period of transition, you should give yourself a chance to get through the process without outside distractions.

This will help you to truly focus on yourself and find the answers that you need. During this time, it is important to remember that not everyone will understand what you are going through. You will have your own thoughts and emotions to deal with, so you don't need any outside distractions. You may feel like you have a lot on your plate right now but try not to worry about it too much. Give yourself time to adjust and focus on getting through the transition period. If you are having trouble adjusting, reach out to a loved one for support. You can also consider talking to someone who has gone through a similar situation, or even seeking therapy. The transition period may feel like it is taking forever, but it will pass. You will get through this difficult time, and everything will be okay.

TIME
IS
TICKING

Time is ticking away, ticking away from me, from you, from us.
Each day time passes, we lose moments and seconds that will never return.

Why are we so worried about the things that are none of our concern?
Why do we worry about the things that we cannot control?

Live your life to the fullest without regrets and understand that you only fail
if you never try.

This life will pass you by if you let it, so love hard, learn from it and then love hard again.
Don't allow this world to stop you from loving.

Don't get so caught up in the matrix that you lose yourself by forgetting yourself through
the lenses of someone else.

That world is not real, and it will leave you stranded in a place where time and space
disappear then longing for that time you lost to reappear.

Time is ticking away in this world but not the next, use your time wisely on this earth cause
who knows when you'll have the opportunity to return.

Remember what they are saying and doing is none of your concern. Don't make other
people's burdens your burdens. They are not yours to bear and having peace in this life
should not be so rare.

Handle yourself with care, take a deep breath forgive yourself and release all the things that
don't serve you and release the people who no longer deserve you.

Time is ticking away in this world for those who choose to not live in the moment, for those
who bear the burdens of others, for those that allow their past to dictate their future.

Time is ticking for those who'd rather dream than do, for those who are more afraid of
failure than success, for those who allow the world to control their narrative.

Time is ticking away.

SAVE
YOURSELF

Continuing to water something that's dead won't change the circumstance. Giving all your breath to situations that are dead only leaves you gasping for air, leaving you on the brink of death because you thought saving them would save you, too.

You must protect yourself at all costs, be vigilant and never leave your mental and emotional essence in the hands of someone who doesn't know the beauty of your essence as you do.

Your mind and heart should not be a battleground for love and security. You should not be fighting to maintain stability between you and another. Love should be a place of peace and serenity, a place where your mind is at ease and you're not in a constant state of worry.

Don't let the heartache and pain from past relationships caused by those who are broken harden your heart and keep you from embracing your worthiness of love from another who is willing to love you to the highest divinity.

Keep your heart open for your God sends that which will be sent from the heavens and the universe. Once you understand that, God will send you everything you ask for as long as you trust the process.

Stop pouring yourself into broken and cracked vessels that will never take initiative to mend. You have to mend yourself and learn to pour into yourself so no one else has to. You don't have to wait on the pouring rain to fill your cup.

Your time on this earth is precious and wasting your time and energy on a time waster will only leave you wishing for that time you lost to reappear so that you can stop the clock before that situation ever began. Redirect your path so that you could stay in the clear.

Love yourself to save yourself and allow grace to heal you. Look within you to find you and in this place, peace will comfort you. You are worthy of the love you want and desire but first you must love yourself entirely.

RELEASE

Sometimes you just have to let it out the best way you know how. Scream, cry, heck break something but once you release it never pick it back up again.

R
E
L
E
A
S
E

Release me from these generational curses placed upon me without any regard or remorse. Curses all of you, who came before me, decided to ignore.

Release me from the trauma you brought into my life because you couldn't control yourself, placing your desires above your morals. Release me from your inability to realize you were the problem.

Release me from the cosmic karma of my past lives that never allowed me to break the reoccurring cycles that hindered me from breaking free for centuries.

Release me from the self-doubt embedded in me from a world that never knew me but wanted to consume me.

Release me from self-sabotage because I thought I didn't deserve better.

Release me from the internalized hate I buried down inside of me because you used me as a pawn in your life games for your own personal gains.

Release me from manipulative love, hypocritical, narcissistic, controlling love because that's not love, nor will it ever be love.

Release me from all the internalized emotional pain that has drained me into submission for years, leaving me in an ocean full of tears.

Release me from the entanglement of my past thoughts and memories that has afflicted me since I was child so that little girl can once again smile.

I release myself so that I can break free from everything that I once knew so, let me go and leave me be in this freedom of peace and prosperity.

TRANSFORM

Just like the caterpillar, I had to stop eating and drinking the illusions of this world causing me confusion.

Just like the caterpillar, I had to remove myself from the world and find peace within my solitude.

I had to walk through the darkest of places in my heart and soul to relinquish all control, to gain control of my demons that have been playing tricks on my mind, twisted my heart and darkened my soul.

Just like the caterpillar, I had to let go of the self I once knew to become the person I am supposed to.

I had to transform, make the transition from the darkness to the light by getting uncomfortable with myself to get comfortable with myself.

Just like the caterpillar, I had to break free of my past and release myself from the tumultuous cycles that have kept me stuck for far too long and realize I am the light that shines bright.

Just like the caterpillar, I transform into a butterfly full of life and love, spreading my wings and flying free above the self-doubt and unworthiness above all the self-pity and shame, above all the sadness and grief.

Transition is not easy and not without struggle, but we must go through the storm in order to grow.

Face your fears because liberation is only a breath away.

LET
IT
GO

Bottled up inside is anger and fury suppressed deep within this eternal vessel.

As life shakes and stirs the spirit the pressure builds, feeling
the tightness increase.

All that is longed for is peace, peace and serenity to the spirit and soul.

Step into solitude and take control for life is a beautiful mess but left
untamed it will consume you and diminish your life force.

So, in the here and now show up for yourself and know the peace is just
a breath away.

Inhale and exhale, inhale and exhale, inhale peace, exhale the torment you
have lived in for so long and change the frequency you have been operating
in, rise to a higher state of vibration.

Align yourself with the light and love that you have always possessed.

To heal you must allow yourself to feel the hurt and pain you endured
over the years.

Let the tears wash it away.
Let go as you let go of the old.

You are golden and your light shines bright even in the darkest of night.

Never revert back to the old or let these worldly illusions corrupt your soul.

LET
IT
GO
PT. 2

You got to let it go.
When it's over, it's over.
You got to let it go.

From your mind, body, soul.
Stop trying to hold on to something that's been dead and gone.

You are carrying around dead weight that don't equate with your purpose.
Wondering why you're feeling tired, barely staying above the surface.

You keep sacrificing yourself to keep the peace for them when they refuse to keep
the peace for you.

You've got to let it go and all that came with it. Stop trying to hold on to what was
and should've been and just place it all where it should have been once it was over.
Taken out along with all the other trash.

Yes, letting go can be hard when there are feelings involved but you have to let it
go in order to evolve and place a lock on the door, so it doesn't revolve.

No need to try to force something that is no longer there when they don't even care
in the first place. It's just about them and maintaining control of your space.

No time for the back and forth, it's time to redirect your course so, drop what is
dead and bury it deep, send it to its maker and go live in peace.

FREQUENCY

Close your eyes, breathe in deep and slowly exhale.
Allow your mind, body and soul to expand and just be.

You are in transition. It is time to face the shadows that lurk in your subconscious.

Get your energy in motion to tackle the untamed emotions of self-doubt and unworthiness
you've been feeling.

I know that these aren't easy dealings, but you must set yourself in the silence, be still,
hold the space and listen.

It's time to adjust and tune into a different frequency from which you have
been operating in.

Keep calm as you settle into the 417 frequencies.
This is where you will clear the inner and outer negativity and subconscious blockages that
have been hindering you, for it seems like an eternity.

Understand this won't be easy because these lower frequencies are very
reactive when stirred.

Please adhere to these cautionary words cause pride, anger, fear, guilt and shame have no
shame, they will have you believing you're the blame so be steadfast and let the trauma go.

Transition into the 528 and restore your equilibrium.

You've been operating in an unease state of mind.
Realize you are a divine being that radiates light and love and remember the love that you
seek starts from within.

Affirm yourself daily and watch your beautiful bloom into its purpose.
Flow into the 741 and awaken your intuition.

Tune into your inner being.
Allow the solitude of silence to speak to your soul source.
Listen with intention.
Keep your focus.
Let it guide you on this journey of self-discovery.
Let it help you decipher between the worldly illusions that try to misappropriate your
energy and light causing confusion and a disconnection from your true self and purpose.

You must protect your energy at all costs.
Have gratitude in all that comes to you while being present in the moment.

Understand that life is forever changing, and love, joy, and peace starts from within.
Patience is your teacher and forgiveness is your healer.

ME

Stepping into the new me.
I don't give 2 cents if you don't like what you see.
I understand this is not what you're use to but I'm now living in my truth.

I took the time to focus on me and removed all the people, places and things that had been hindering me and if you can't take the time to get to know the new me, you can keep on walking right on pass me.

I no longer put myself on the back burner by putting your needs before mine. I had to learn the hard way I can't heal you and me at the same time so, I choose me.

Yes, I had to be selfish in order to give myself the best of me. The time, patience, and care in order to nurture and heal me.

You didn't care to see the shadows I had to fight to find me, you just wanted what you wanted from me even if it was at the demise of me so, I don't give 2 cents cause I don't need your 2 cents.

I'm going to keep on walking while you keep on talking that nonsense on how I used to be, supposed to be presently in this moment but in this moment, this is me.

Take me or leave me but remember when you see me to keep that same energy and walk on by.

Stepping into the new me and I don't give 2 grains of sand if you don't like what you see cause this is me and I am loving me to infinity.

SAY WHAT YOU WANT

I'm tired of the superficial people in this world trying to tear me down with their melodramatic illusions of self and how they are better than.

It's sad that being yourself is the toughest when you are living in a world of the many changing faces.

Well, to hell with it all.
I know I'm different from the way I talk and walk.
I even stutter at times when I speak and I have a dap harder than some guys, but I've been walking like this since I was five.

I'm proud to be different no need to live up to anyone's standards but mine. I see life through light and color and walk to the rhythm in my head. That's why you'll never meet another; I'm uniquely made.

So, call me what you want as I pay you no mind.
I'll walk with my head up knowing you have no power over me cause you walking just as blinded as me.

In the end we are all liars, hypocrites, and procrastinators. So, I stay tone deaf to the haters as they continue to sit on the sideline and be spectators.

Remember what's done in the dark will come to the light cause we all have shadows inside we battle on a daily.

So, say what you want as I continue to walk in my purpose with my gap tooth smile and all. No need for me to even speak as you work on your own downfall in front of me.

I
N
F
I
N
I
T
E

My energy is infinite
My eternal power is infinite
I flow like rivers through valleys into the ever-flowing sea

Step by step I molt and shed the old and unworthy that serves my spirit no
purpose and doesn't enlighten me

My growth is infinite
My soul is infinite
Beyond this world and the next
Beyond time and space

My longitude and latitude have no boundaries
Can't fit me in your box of delusional lies cause I'm walking in my
truth and purpose

My light is infinite
My inner love is infinite
Purposeful and abundant

Never again will I allow someone to make me feel like I don't deserve it

Never finite

I am an infinite being with infinite possibilities with an inner peace that can't be
bought or stolen

ROYAL

Be proud, be bold, be you, be Royal. Do you and forget the rest.

GIVING LIFE TO YOUR LIFE

Wake up, and take control of the life you've been given and make it whole. It's time to stop sleepwalking through the days and start living with purpose, in every way.

You have the power to give life to your life. Light up the darkness and banish the strife and find the beauty in the smallest things.

The joy that fills us, when we let love in. It's in the tears we shed, when we let ourselves feel and the courage we find, when we decide to heal.

It starts with a dream, a vision, a goal. Something that sets fire to your soul, something that makes you feel alive and pushes you forward, into the light.

But it's not just about the destination it's about the journey, and the transformation it's about the steps you take, day by day to create the life you want, and find your way.

So, don't wait for the world to come to you It's up to you to make your dreams come true Take a step forward, and don't look back and give your life the power it deserves, no matter what you think you lack.

Don't let fear hold you back from your dreams. Take a chance and take the lead. Believe in yourself, and never give up and make the most of every moment.

Let go of fears and break through self-imposed limits. Believe in your strength, and the beauty within it. Practice gratitude, and savor life's simple pleasures. Let your heart sing, with the freedom of your treasures.

So, go out there and give life to your life. Embrace the beauty of the world and make it yours. For you have the power to create, to change, to grow and with every breath, let your life's energy flow.

Don't wait for the world to come to you. It's up to you to make your dreams come true. At time it won't be easy, and there will be days when the road seems dark, and you're lost in the maze or feel jaded by the world's crazy; but don't give up, and don't give in, for you have the power within to win.

So, give life to your life, and let it shine. Let your heart lead, and your soul align with the Divine.

LATE BLOOMER

I may have started late, but I'll bloom eventually.

Late bloomer, they called me, as they watched others blossom, I waited in the shadow of their wings. Sometimes feeling out of place, like I didn't belong, watching others flourish while I struggled in place.

There were days when I felt left behind. When others seemed to have it all, and I struggled to find my own place, my own niche, my own purpose within this life.

Through time and grace, I learned to embrace my journey, my pace to trust in my own timing, to find my own space.

Patiently I knew my time would come, when the world was ready to see the beauty that laid within and the gifts I had yet to develop.

So, I waited with grace, as the seasons turned and passed, I didn't worry about time. I knew my path was different, my journey winding, my pace slow, but moving forward, and that's all I needed to know.

For every setback, there was a lesson to learn. For every obstacle, a chance to discern. What truly matters, what's worth fighting for, what makes my heart sing, what ignites my core.

As I grew older, I began to see, that being a late bloomer was not a tragedy. For every missed opportunity, there was a new door, a chance to explore and find what I was looking for inside of me.

I trust that my path will continue to align. Don't count me out or underestimate me. I'm a force to be reckoned with and I'm not done yet.

So, I'll keep on growing, at my own pace. With each day, I'll continue to shine bright as I bloom in my own time, in my own light as my petals open with beautiful grace.

Embrace your journey and take your time. For being a late bloomer can be just fine. It's not about being the first to bloom or competing in their race. It's about finding your own way, your own path and blooming in your own time, free from comparison trap this world defines.

When spoken with intention you will open up a new world without restrictions. Know that you are and will always be what you speak. You hold the power within to speak life into you, speak life into your destiny and bring it to the light.

I AM GRATEFUL
I AM STRONG
I AM LOVE AND THE LOVE THAT IS WITHIN ME
I AM SUCCESSFUL IN ALL THAT I SAY AND DO
I AM WORTHY OF LOVE AND ALL THAT IS GOOD
I AM PEACE
I AM THE LIGHT THAT SHINES BRIGHT
I AM OPEN TO WHAT THIS WORLD HAS TO OFFER
I AM BEAUTIFULLY MADE
I AM RADIANT
I AM THE WORDS I THINK AND SPEAK
I AM A CREATIVE FORCE
I AM INFINITE WITH INFINITE POSSIBILITIES
I AM PROSPEROUS
I AM UNIQUE
I AM HEALED
I AM ENERGY IN ITS PUREST FORM
I AM POWERFUL
I AM A REFLECTION OF THE DIVINE
I AM DIVINE
I AM INTELLIGENT
I AM ABUNDANT
I AM FOCUSED ON MY PURPOSE
I AM BLESSED BEYOND MEASURE
I AM WEALTH
I AM MORE THAN ENOUGH
I AM DETERMINED
I AM CAPABLE OF WHAT I SET MY MIND TO
I AM LIMITLESS
I AM WHO I SAY I AM
I AM XKWIZIT

I
A
M

LOVE
NOTES

NOTES

This is universal, it can make you smile, and it can make you cry, and it can bring us together. Notes can provide inspiration; notes can give us strength to push through the hard times and can make us fall in love

I have always tried to lead with love—I believe it is the only way to stay grounded. Let love be your guide and reject hate even when it seems the most convenient option. Love is the only thing that can heal us, it is also the only thing that can make you feel whole again after a traumatic event. Love is a powerful force that can heal any wound, and it's the only thing that will help you move forward. Love is the only thing that can bring you peace and happiness in life. Love is a feeling that makes you feel good about yourself, it changes your perspective on things, and it makes you appreciate all the little things in life.

Love is what love does. Love shows truth when you're surrounded by a room full of lies. It's what gives you hope when all seems lost. Love is the sun that shines on your darkest days, it's the rain that falls on those who are sad. Love is a ray of light in the darkness, it's the rainbow after a storm.

Being vulnerable and showing love is often considered a sign of weakness, but it's also a sign of strength. It takes courage to show your true self, especially when you know that someone could leave because of it. Love isn't always easy or comfortable, but it's worth it in the end.

Love makes me sing, love is where my dreams come true, love is where colors collide to create the indigo sky. Love is where the sun hides when it wants to play hide and seek, love is where the moon dances in the night sky. Love is where the ocean sings a song of love, where it touches the sky, love is found where the rivers flow. Love is where the mountains rest, love is where the trees grow. Love requires no words to be spoken.

I will continue to remain open to love in all its forms. I will allow myself to be loved, and I will give my love freely.

CAN YOU SEE ME

Can you see me?
Can you see me now?

I am here standing right in front of you Bare naked.
See I already stripped before I even knocked on your door.
But you're standing there with your eyes closed, blinded by what you think love should be. But tonight, I'm going to take everything you thought love was and should be and turn it into passionate mind, body and soul therapy.

So, I told you to strip for me.
You tell me you're afraid.
You have nothing to lose except for that excess baggage of insecurity and deceit that your past lives have placed upon you.

So, I began to unbutton your issues of self-doubt and trust.
Unzipped the many lies you were ever told.

Now that you are stripped clean, I began to rub your body down with oils of trust commitment and understanding.

And as I massage your body you release every single emotional storm through your body trembles and through your tears have now released all of your fears.

For the first time you are able to trust and for the first time you have opened up your eyes and saw true liberation standing in front of you looking you right in the eye telling you the truth.

Now your soul can embark on a journey where your soul will become united with another and for the first time in your life you let your heart roam among the stars.

Your eyes become the moon lighting up the darkness which has once blinded you and your soul becomes one with the sun which is drawing in all the earth's energy and for the first time in your life you are able to see yourself for the strong-willed black goddess you really are.

And I look into your eyes, and I ask you can you see me? Can you see me now?

Good.

LOVERS
&
FRIENDS

I want to be more than just lovers and friends.
I want to be your backbone and support system.
Provide you with nothing more than what you deserve.

I want to be the sun that brings you joy and
the moon that watches over you at night.
I want to give you my all so that you can shine like
the brightest light.

I'll be your strength when you are weak and your eyes when are unable to see. Now
this is what lovers and friends mean to me.

Walking and talking together while sharing our souls with each other.
This that type of love that makes you dream in color. This the kind of love that makes
you feel like anything is possible together.

You sparkle and shine like the stars in the sky.
When I'm with you I stay on a natural high. This that type of love that makes you
never have to wonder or ever want to say goodbye.

It's that check yes or no box butterfly feeling in your stomach when you look into my
eyes knowing in your heart, I would never do anything to put our love in compromise
or lead to our demise.

Loving and supporting each other into greatness.
Understanding this love is a once in a lifetime love and we don't want to waste it.
Cherishing the moments as partners not opponents.
Being each other's light when we find ourselves in darkness.
This is what lovers and friends means to me.

TYPE
OF
LOVE

Going in, out of consciousness.
Breathing in and out of us.
I don't know where this is going but I know that this is love.

Got me drifting on cosmic clouds with a love I can't deny. This goes beyond
space and time.
This that type of love that goes beyond the basic frame of mind.
This that type of love that's so very hard to find.

This love is eternal, full of beauty and wonder. We vowed to never let this
world come between us or take us under.

Never knew a love so sweet, it's knocking me off my feet, don't care if I'm
in too deep.
That selfish type of love, you can keep.

This love is like the sun and moon, like summer rain in the afternoon, like a
cool breeze in the middle of June.

Going in, out of consciousness.
Breathing in and out of us.
I don't know where this is going but I know that this is love.

B L U E

S K I E S

Blue skies on my mind.
Blue skies on my mind.
Blue skies on my mind and I'm feeling fine.

It's a lovely da y outside with the sunshining on my face.
Moving at my own pace ain't trying to run no race.
I'm going to stay focused on my path and keep my heart and mind open on this journey to
which I will embrace.

I keep my vision 2 0 / 2 0 on me, myself and I and though we may cross paths I was never
meant to walk yours or you mine's so focus on you and I'm a do me.
Breathe in deep and know what will be will be.

I'm going to let my little light shine cause I walk in the light, I talk in the light and now
that I am walking in my purpose no one can ever dim my light.

That's why I got blue skies on my mind and I'm feeling fine.

No longer worried about the past.
Just trying to create memories that will last lifetimes but, in the meantime

I go with the flow and it's Ok to say no, and remember my peace is scared and through
darkness I have made it, so I won't let no one disrupt the peace I have created.

That's why I got blue skies on my mind and I'm feeling fine.

I point to myself and say I love you.
I am worthy, and I am light brightening up the darkest of nights cause I am joy, I am
peace, and no one will ever love you like me.

I hug myself and I say Asé and
I continue on my day with blue skies on my mind.

I see heaven in your eyes.
I see stars when you smile.
You're my angel and I'm so grateful.

You are the essences of beauty.
Even when you're mad you still a cutie.

A

Your inner soul is graceful like butterflies in the springtime, and I am
grateful that you are mine so, go and let your light shine.

N

Our connection is pure and true, I just want to be next to you. Even
through the ups and downs I want our love to stand the test of time.

G

Time and space don't exist in your eyes. I get lost in your galactic
universe, mesmerized by your elegant nature.
You are marvelous works completed by the creator.

E

Your heart is home and where peace resides and when my days are in
turmoil and chaos is in my head, you take me by the hand, hold me close
to soothe my soul.

You created a safe space for me to express my truest self.

L

You are love and love is within you that's why.
I see heaven in your eyes.
I see stars when you smile.
You're my angel and I'm so grateful.

YOUNG / SO (acrostic)

You make me feel so young.
You make me feel so young.
You brighten up my day in a very special way.

This love I can't compare.
Came out of nowhere.
Caught me by surprise.
So sweet it makes me want to cry.

I'm grateful for you and all the things that you do.
Keep a smile on my face and I just want to say.

You make me feel so young.
You make me feel so young.
You brighten up my day in a very special way.

I don't want this feeling to go away.
I want this to last forever, babe, just take my hand and we'll fly away you and me
together forever, babe.

You make me feel so young.
You make me feel so young.
You brighten up my day in a very special way.

AS YOU HOLD MY HAND

As I open my eyes to a new day, I look at my life and see how far I have come.

Through the cloudy days, crying at night, heartache and pain.

Through my eyes you can see my trials and tribulations not knowing if I was strong enough to make it another day. Running from myself trying to find myself.

Feeling like the world is on my shoulders like boulders, I try to stand strong.

I look up to the sky asking, "Why, Lord? Why?" Like many times before and as the rain falls upon my face, I'm not sure of what tomorrow may bring.

Now that the storm is over all I know is that tomorrow will be a new day.

A new day for me to know that the path you made for me is the same path that will test me then bless me.

As I walk through the shadows, I know you will do what you say you will do.

I began my journey with you by my side and as you hold my hand, I know that everything will be alright. With every step I take you will be there, today and tomorrow just as you were yesterday.

HYDRATE

Confusion in my head as I sit here exhausted from this.
Feels like deep down inside I've lost it all.
Somewhere between life and who I'd rather not name.
It feels like I have been spinning on a merry-go-round non-stop for some time.

Dizzy and lightheaded from the lack of oxygen that has been depleted from my lungs.

Unable to move, fatigued, from all the fighting, lying and backbiting. My muscles start to fail, sight blurry. Someone please lift this veil. I'm finding it harder and harder to function in this mess.

In a manipulated state, I've found myself in. Again and again, I find myself starting to drift.

My respiration is shallow like their lack of emotion, and no compassion.
As I lay here disoriented and thirsty, I pray to God that he rescues me
from this dehydration.

I am on the verge of a heat stroke. All because they fail to disclose vital information about their lack of cooperation.

Drinking on the wrong things can deplete your system. Now I'm dehydrated because I chose to overlook what I was consuming.

Dehydrated from unspoken words.
Dehydrated from lack of emotional support.
Dehydrated from the lack of truth.

So, I lay here praying for relief as I start to let go. But you — yes you! — came out of nowhere and quenched my thirst.

You lifted my head and told me to drink. Drink of your truth, so that I could see the real you and the truth that you bring.

You told me to drink. Drink of your communication, and my dehydration from unspoken words would be no more. Assuring me all vital information would be known. I felt your liquid sincerity to my core.

So, I continue to drink of the pure things to break the cycle of doubt and distrust. I drink of the pure things to break the cycle of uncertainty and lack of support.

I drink to replenish my mentality so that we can communicate all relevant formalities because absorption of each other's mental is far more important than absorption of our physical.

Dehydrated no longer, my strength returns and along with strength comes understanding.

Confusion no more. I see the truth like never before. I look into your eyes and tell you to drink.

Drink of my truth and hydrate.
Drink of my communication and hydrate.
Drink of my emotional support and hydrate.
We drink together, never to be dehydrated again.

SLOW DANCE

Slow dance with me.
You are so sweet.
Just take my hand and just come with me.
I never met anyone like you.
You give love that is so pure and true, no one could ever love me the way that you do.
Gentle and sweet, if you were a song, I would play you on repeat.

My gratitude for you is faithful.
The way you carry yourself is so graceful.
I won't be wasteful with this love.
I want to nurture this love.
I want you to know I love everything about you.

I don't want this to ever end. Can we just stay here and look adoringly into each other's eyes as we sway to the melodies of our hearts and souls? Can you feel our love taking control with the sweetest symphony I have ever heard?

Loving you has been a pleasure. I can see us dancing to this love song forever with you by my side in this life and the next.

C
O
C
O
A

Cocoa smooth like butter on melanated skin, A sight that always draws me in. The way it glows in the ray of sunlight, makes my heart skip a beat.

It's like a dance of light and dark, A contrast that leaves its mark. Soft and supple, like a rose petal, It's a sight that's truly unforgettable.

Cocoa smooth like butter, a natural delight, Nourishing and moisturizing, day and night. It brings out the best in our skin, smooth and supple. Do I need to say it again?

Melanated skin, a gift to behold. A canvas of beauty, a story untold. From golden honey to dark espresso, Each shade unique, each one a manifesto.

So, let your beauty shine, unapologetically bold. Embrace your melanated skin as you shine like gold. For you are a queen, a goddess supreme, a melanated beauty, a vision of a dream.

Melanated skin, a masterpiece divine. A canvas that glows with a hue so fine. Your presence is a celebration of life, a testament to your strength and favor from the Divine.

NEW
BEGININGS

NEW BEGINNINGS

We will all experience new
beginnings. As we grow and learn,
there will always be something new
to experience, so embrace this life
with open arms., so embrace this
life with open arms.

New beginnings are just that: new beginnings. They are times when we have to clear out the old and make room for the new. They are times when we must be willing to let go of what no longer serves us so that we can welcome in what does. They are like the morning after a storm. New beginnings are like new leaves on a branch in springtime. They say that every ending is also a beginning, and this is true for every life situation as well.

It is only when we are willing to let go of the past, so that we can make room for the future, that we can move forward. We must be willing to let go of old ways of thinking and doing things if we want anything new in our lives. We are all on a journey that has no end, and our lives are like the seasons—they change. We go through cycles of birth, growth, decay and death. This is what it means to be human.

We are constantly evolving into more complex beings. Our minds, bodies and spirits are always changing as we adapt to new situations and environments. We are always growing, even when it seems that things are not working out for us. So, when we are in the midst of change, we can feel like we're being torn apart. This is because all things must pass, including our old ways of thinking and doing things. Whenever there is a shift in consciousness, it brings with it a feeling of loss that precedes the gain. We may feel like something has been taken from us (even though nothing has).

And when we are in the midst of change, we may feel like we're being torn apart. This is because all things must pass, including our old ways of thinking and doing things. So, welcome this new phase in your life, and be open to the things you will learn from it.

A chance to start anew to let go of the past and embrace what's true, a time to shed the old and explore new things. Leave behind what's holding us back and step into the future, with courage and with every breath we take, a new chapter unfolds a story yet to be written. We have the power to create and shape our fate to dance to our own beat and embrace what's great within.

New beginnings, a chance to start anew. A blank page, a fresh canvas, what will you do? It's time to let go of what's holding you back. The past is behind you and the future is waiting, so plant your seeds and watch them grow with patience and love; let your new life flow.

Take the leap and take it now; it's your time to shine, your time is now. Embrace the unknown and let your fears subside. So, take a deep breath, and jump right in, leave the past behind and move ahead. Chase your dreams and face your fears and lay them to bed.

New beginnings are a time to grow.

It's never too late to start anew, to chase your dreams, and make them come true, to find your voice, and speak your truth.

C
H
A
N
G
E

Change is ok.
Change is ok.

Our world is forever changing.
Our lives are forever changing.
Change is inevitable.
You can't hate change and want things to change at the same time, you will find
yourself fighting unnecessary battles.

You can't stop change from happening so open yourself and embrace the journey
and release everything that has been holding you back and go with the flow.

Realign your mind and say,
I embrace change within me and around me.
I am open and free flowing in change.
I embrace change with open arms.
Change is ok.
Change is ok.

Don't let the fear of change keep you bound and chained in a cycle of stagnation
that has been keeping you from becoming you.

Embrace the change happening within you and around you. Free flow into that
change and accept it with open arms.

NEW
LIGHT

I fought and survived the darkest nights now I see myself in a new light. I see my future is very bright.

This was no 4-leaf clover. I had to get in the direction of my destiny, run over any doubts that had me questioning myself and my ability to achieve what was inside of me.

You can call me an over-comer even though it took many moons and summers to discover that I am light, and light is within me.

I appreciate my mother for never giving up on me her daughter, even though it wasn't easy raising someone with emotions like raging waters.

Walking with my head held high a twinkle in my smile and sparks in my eyes, I rise to new heights unseen. I guess it's just that thoroughbred gene that lets me know I can do anything I set my mind to, stay true to myself and let my strength and endurance carry me through.

Never again will I want to tap out early on this journey. No matter how many times the world tries to cut me down I will stand strong on this solid foundation I built and wear my crown.

I fought and survived the darkest of nights. I'm not going to let no one determine who I am. This is my story and this story I'm a write.

LEARN
YOU
SOMETHING

Come. Sit down. Let me learn you something.
Open up your mind and let me teach you something.

It's time to unlearn, relearn and over-learn everything you were ever taught.
You know this is that deep thought knowledge, different from everything
you ever known about.

This is deeper than what your current intellect can comprehend. Don't get
so caught up in your quest for the truth, you lose your grounding and get
hoodwinked and bamboozled by the fakes that pretend to be. Find yourself
and never allow yourself to be caught in a trend is key.

See, we are souls born into a vessel that we are supposed to have and hold,
love and cherish from that day forward, for better or for worse, through
sickness and health until death do you part.

That's why you must be careful of what you consume through your oculars
because your eyes are the gateway to you. You must go within yourself to
find the answers you seek, understand this journey is not for the weak.

Sit down and let me learn you something, you will have to face the hard
truth that we all been completely lied to.

Your soul is not a separate entity from you, your soul is you and what your
body feels is a physical manifestation of what you as the soul is
experiencing. When you say your soul is restless and tired that means you
are restless and tired, when your soul is crying out, you are crying out and
when your soul is happy you are happy.

It's a lot to take in but I need you to start thinking beyond the physical and
tap into you, the spiritual being that you are and unlock your mind. This
journey of self-discovery won't be easy, but it will be worth it.

The ways of this world were taught to us by design so that we could forget
our true selves over time to keep us in line and disconnect from the Divine.

Come. Sit down and let me learn you something. Open up your mind and
let me teach you something.

POWER OF THE TONGUE

With every word that leaves our lips. A powerful force, that never quits. A tool of creation, or of destruction. A double-edged sword, with no instruction.

The tongue, a weapon of great might. A tool of darkness, or of light. It can build up, or tear down. It can lift up or cause us to drown.

Words can heal or leave a scar or open and leave a wound that may never heal. A word of kindness, or a seed of hope. It can lift us up, when we can't cope.

The tongue, a tool of great power. A gift we must use with great honor. A voice that can bring forth change. A force that can bring joy or pain.

Use your tongues, with great care. To bring about love, and not despair. To bring hope, and not fear. To bring about peace, and not to destroy.

With every word that you say, let us use our tongues to speak life in a positive way. Speak with love, and not hate. Speak with understanding, and not chaos. Speak to uplift, and not to put down. Speak with prosperity and not failure.

So, remember to mind your tongue for the power of the tongue is great.

THE WATCHERS

Even in our darkest hour
remember we have those that
watch over us. We are never
alone. Keep fighting, keep
pushing and never give up.

FULL OF WONDER

Life is full of wonder that leads to many questions and when searching for those answers you will learn many lessons.

Keep an open heart and mind, don't let this world swayed you or jade you.

Live life to the fullest and watch yourself become unstoppable in your quest to greatness.

Hold no hatred in your heart and let the Divine take care of the rest while you let your mind rest.

Never let no one dim your light, those who doubt you will be blinded by your magnificent brilliance.

No need to keep up with appearances; you walk to the beat of your own drum that's why you already won.

Life is full of wonder that leads to many questions and when searching for those answers you will learn many lessons.

Stay focused on your path, beware of the charmers. They are only here to disarm you and take full advantage of you.

Keep your armor on tight and be ready to fight because they love to come in the darkness of night.

Keep an open heart but don't let everybody in. Protect your sacred space from those who just want to play around and roam without putting any work in.

Life is full of wonder so go live your life and live it to the fullest without regret.

This life is yours and yours alone leave the past behind and let no one dictate your present or future.

Experience what this beautiful life has to offer and continue to be full of wonder.

YOU ARE ENOUGH

You are more than enough.
You are more than what this world thinks of you.
Your energy is breathtaking, and you are more than amazing.
You are depth layered in grace.

This world will never see you the way that you do. Hold your head high to the sky and never ask or wonder why because you are uniquely made in the image of the most high dipped in melanin and kissed by the sun.

Walk at your own pace you don't have to join a race that was never made for you in the first place and give yourself some grace.

Stay true to yourself and give this world what it has been missing, you. There will never be another you so again to yourself remain true.

Dare to be you even when you feel misunderstood.
Dare to be you when no one is cheering you on.
Dare to be you even when you don't feel like being you because you are enough.

You are the breath that breathes life into everything you touch.
You are that light that shines when you walk into a room. No need for you to dress up and put on a mask and a costume.
You are the flowers that bloom in the springtime. You have been amazing since you were birthed from the womb.

Walk in the purity of your grace and make sure you leave your trace in this world because you, my dear, could never be duplicated or replaced.

You are more than enough just the way you are, so walk with pride and let them marvel at the rhythm and flow in your stride.

PURPOSE

As I walk upon this path, I feel a sense of clarity. My purpose now in focus, it's become my true focus with every step I take, I feel my heart begin to soar and with each passing moment, I know I'm meant for more.

Walking in my purpose, I'm on a journey guided by my divine intuition. It's a feeling so sublime I know that I am destined for greatness. It's my fate and knowing that every step I take, I'm one step closer to my destiny.

I've found my true calling, and it fills me up inside. No longer just willing to survive, I'm living and thriving in my passion which is my purpose, it's the fuel that drives me on the path of discovery, and I'll never be deterred again from what has been destined for me.

I'm grateful for this journey, for the lessons along the way, and I'll keep walking in my purpose. With the wind at my back, I know I'll never lack because no one could ever take what has been divinely given.

I'm in alignment with my destiny. It's a feeling so surreal and as I continue on this journey, I know I'll face some strife, but I'll keep on walking, because I'm meant to live this life.

So, if you're feeling lost, and your purpose is unclear, just keep on walking forward, and you'll find it will appear. Trust in your intuition, and let it guide your way, you'll find your purpose in due time, and you'll live it every day. Use your purpose as your guide, and never lose sight, keep on walking with pride towards a future that is filled with light.

Walking in my purpose, I'm on a journey guided by my divine intuition. It's a feeling so sublime I know that I am destined for greatness. It's my fate and knowing that every step I take, I'm one step closer to my destiny.

FREE

I want to live free, unbound by chains, I want to break free from society's constraints to let my voice be heard and my spirit soar, to live my life and not be another metaphor. Living free, living wild not afraid to be myself, living brave and taking on this world.

I refuse to let fear hold me back to be a prisoner of my own mind, I'll take chances and seize the day. No more "what ifs" to get in my way.

I'll dance in the rain and sing to the sky, I'll spread my wings and not be afraid to fly. I'll laugh out loud, love with my heart and leave my mark for the world to discover.

My spirit will always be free. Break free from the chains of conformity and live life on my own terms, be my own authority.

Living free is about embracing the unknown and finding the strength in the things we don't yet understand, it's about walking my own path, even when it's lonely and there is no one to hold my hand. It's about trusting myself, even when I'm the only one willing to take a stand.

Living free means embracing my uniqueness, acknowledging my flaws and how far I have come. It means taking risks and making mistakes. For every fall is a chance to awake to the possibility of what I can create and the power I have to shape my fate.

Living free is not a solo endeavor. It's finding those who lift us higher who encourage us to be bolder and braver, supporting us through the ups and downs, cheering us on through the smiles and frowns and reminding us that we are not bound to the limits that society has tried to crown but keeps us grounded as we wear our crown.

So, let's live life unapologetically with open hearts and minds, and compassion. In living free we find serenity and a life filled with endless possibility and passion.

DON'T FORGET

We chase the stars and reach for the sky, and dream of the big things that make us high. The grand goals that fuel our ambition and give us a sense of life's mission.

But in the rush to reach the top, we forget the things that make our hearts stop. The little moments we can't rewind, the small pleasures we often find.

We lose ourselves in the daily grind and overlook the treasures we can find. The beauty in a sunset's hue, the simple joy of a morning dew.

The gentle touch of a loved one's hand, the warmth of the sun on a winter's day, the warmth of sunshine on our face, the love that a simple hug can seal. Moments in time we can all embrace so don't allow them to go to waste.

We get caught up in the daily grind. The rush and stress that cloud our minds. The big things seem to take control, and leave us feeling empty, hollow.

We forget the simple joys in life, the moments that make us laugh and smile, the feeling of nostalgia only a song can bring.

We forget the way the world can shine, in moments that are truly divine. The way a sunset paint the sky, or a cool breeze that passes by.

So, let us not forget the little things, the tiny moments that give our heart wings. So, take a breath and slow down and enjoy the small things that makes our hearts sing.

BECOMING XKWIZIT

Becoming Xkwizit is a journey that starts within. It's about self-discovery and embracing myself in my own skin. It's about finding the beauty in the things that make you unique and using that to build the confidence you seek. It is a journey that requires dedication, patience, and a willingness to push beyond my limits. It is about discovering and embracing my true self and striving to reach my full potential.

To become Xkwizit, I had to first have a clear understanding of who I am, my strengths, weaknesses, and passions. I had to learn to love myself, flaws and all.

Becoming Xkwizit is not about fitting in with the crowd. It's about standing out, speaking my truth out loud. It's about living authentically and being true to who I am and letting my light shine bright like the stars.

Becoming Xkwizit takes time and patience, too. It's about setting goals and following through, believing in myself and my abilities and not letting doubt or fear cloud your possibilities. So, I took that first step on the road to being Xkwizit because I knew I was worth it. I remind myself daily to love myself and be kind.

One important aspect of becoming Xkwizit is cultivating a sense of gratitude and appreciation for the world around me. This meant taking the time to notice the beauty in my everyday life, to connect with others, and find joy in even the smallest moments.

It required commitment to my personal growth and development. It took me facing and overcoming my fears, stepping outside my comfort zone, and challenging myself to be better every day.

Ultimately, becoming Xkwizit is about living a life of purpose, passion, and meaning. It is about finding one's place in the world and using one's unique talents and abilities to make a positive impact. It is a journey that requires courage, perseverance, and an unwavering commitment to excellence.

FAMILY

Family is how you define it. Family
are the people who love and support
you. Family are those who
encourage you to be the best you

M
A
M
A

Hey, Mama,

Do you realize how special you are? You manifested what you wrote in your yearbook years ago. Two girls two years apart so that they could grow up and have a bond so tight nothing or no one could ever tear them apart. Something you always longed for but never got.

So, you raised us to always love and support each other through the good and bad, confide in each other whether we're angry or sad and to always build each other up no matter what.

You sacrificed so we could have what we wanted and needed, and I know a lot of those sacrifices we didn't even see. You did the best you could with the tools you had, and I want to apologize for the times I made you sad.

I know the way we turned out wasn't guaranteed but I'm glad we became and fulfilled some of your wildest dreams.

Mama, do you know how special you are that the divine saw you and gave you exactly what you asked for? Two girls two years apart who march to the beat of their own drums, who are intelligent and smart, with beautiful spirits and hearts.
Two girls two years apart who love each other beyond measure, who would do anything for each other and wouldn't let nothing or no one come between them because they know they are stronger together.

I hope that we continue to make you proud so you can always carry a smile when you think of us as we live our lives to the fullest just like you told us and despite the things we've been through, I will always love and cherish us, and hold the things you instilled in us close to my heart.

I am grateful to you, and I just want to say thank you for all that you have done for us as a mother.

Love you.

Dear Big Sista,

I want you to know that I am so very proud of you and the things you have accomplished in this life. I see your growth and it shows from the inside out and I know you will reach all your destinations without a shadow of doubt.

You have been someone I have always looked up to, your strength and determination to always push through the darkest of places only shows the resilience in you. You are unapologetically you and that's what I admire most about you, with a presence unmatched.

Your light shines brighter with every day that passes, using life lessons learned to transform into the beautiful, amazing Goddess you are today. Living in your purpose and moving with intention and doing it on purpose that's why your blessings stay coming in as surplus.

You are loving and supportive with a listening ear that never judges. You provide words of encouragement that make me want to conquer this life without fear or the fear of judgment. You remind me that I owe this world nothing but everything to myself and to never lose sight of the light I have inside of me.

This life has not been kind to us, but we never made a fuss even when the world seemed to turn their backs on us, even when people had no confidence in us to be great. We never gave up on each other or let pride and ego get in the way, we pushed each other to be the best that we could be.

I am grateful that we have a bond we can hold on to when it feels like the world is trying to take us under, a bond that creates a shelter and provides us shelter in stormy weather, a bond that will never be broken because we know we are stronger together than we are apart.

I am grateful for you; I am grateful for us. Love you from your little Sista.

Y O U

I thought I knew love before you.
When I met you, you showed me a love that I didn't have to question, constantly
ask or beg for.

You pour into my cup daily without hesitation. It's crazy that someone like you was only a
part of my imagination, a daydream in the afternoon skies with my heart in a constant
longing for someone to love me wholeheartedly without judgment.

You walked into my life with peace as your name and, in your eyes, comfort in your touch
and unconditional love in your heart.
You created a safe place for me to be me.

From the moment we met I realized I traveled several lifetimes to get back to you. Your
love is so pure and true no other love will do.

So, I have to do what is needed to protect you and what we have built at all costs.

You're my lost diamond in the rough and I would travel another thousand lifetimes to get
back to you again.

I will love you each and every day like it's our last cause I understand this physical life is on
loan from the Divine and this is the sweetest love I've ever known.

Never focus on the petty just on a love that is slow and steady, a love that feeds your soul,
helps you become the better version of you without having to pay a toll.

This is a cooperative love not a I'll sit back and watch you put in all the work kinda love.
This is that I truly trust you and never think twice or have to worry kinda love.
That I got you in your most vulnerable moments without judgment love.

Your love is so intentional and pure within your arms I feel secure and without fear.
I know within my heart and soul this love will forever endure another thousand lifetimes.

B
E
S
T
F
R
I
E
N
D

I just wanted to take a moment to tell you how much you mean to me. You're not just a friend, you're my best friend, and that's a title that carries a lot of weight. A true friend is someone who is always there for you, no matter what, and who genuinely cares about your well-being. They are loyal, honest, trustworthy, and supportive, and they are willing to go the extra mile to help you when you need it most.

Over the years, we've been through so much together - from the highs of our biggest accomplishments to the lows of our toughest challenges. Through it all, you've been my constant source of support and laughter. You've seen me at my best and my worst, and you've always been there with a listening ear and a shoulder to lean on.

Thinking back on all of the memories we've made together; I am filled with gratitude and appreciation for the bond we share. From the silly inside jokes, we still laugh about to the deep conversations we've had about life and everything in between, our friendship has been a constant source of support and joy.

I cherish the memories we've made and look forward to all the adventures still to come. I can't imagine navigating this crazy world without you by my side, and I feel incredibly lucky to call you my best friend.

You're not just a friend, you're family. Here's to many more years of laughter, love, and friendship. Thank you for being my best friend.

WITH US

We are never alone. Even when
we feel left out or abandoned.
Those who came before us are
with us every step of the way.

STOLEN TRUTH

What was once stolen will
be found. What was once
hidden will be revealed.

FLOW

Go with the flow. Don't let this life overwhelm you with the things that won't even matter in the end. Open your heart and mind and embrace this life with your arms wide open.

YOU

ARE

XKWIZIT

ABOUT THE AUTHOR

Carmela is a talented artist and writer known for their unique creative vision and thought-provoking works. With a passion for exploring the human experience, Carmela creates art and literature that captures the essence of life in all its complexity.

As a writer, Carmela captures the nuances of the human experience. Their writing style is characterized by a keen observation of detail and a deep understanding of human nature. Carmela's works span a range of genres, from poetry and short stories to novels and essays. No matter the medium, Carmela's writing is always thought-provoking and inspiring.

As an artist Carmela is equally adept at capturing the essences of human spirit. Their works often feature bold, vivid colors and striking imagery that draws the viewer in and invites them to explore deeper. Whether working in abstract or figurative styles, Carmela imbues their art with a deep sense of emotion and a powerful message.

Overall, Carmela is a true creative force, blending their artistic and literary talents into a unique and captivating body of work. Their art and writing are a testament to the power of creative expression and the importance of exploring the world around us.